Musafir

(From Earth to the Heavens)

JagritiTiwari

BookLeaf
Publishing

India | USA | UK

Made with ❤ on the BookLeaf Publishing Platform
www.bookleafpub.in
www.bookleafpub.com

Dedication

I dedicate this collection of poems
to those silent moments
that stayed with me even in darkness ,
that did not let me fall apart ,
but gave me the strength of words
and taught me how to live .

Each poem is a heartbeat of my soul ,
born from the depths of depression ,
yet glowing as a ray of hope .
If these lines can touch
the unspoken pain of someone else ,
that shall be the truest purpose
of my writing .

- Jagriti Tiwari (2004)

Preface

I am a traveller of the earth ,
I keep no longing for the skies .
Whatever gamble fate may play ,
I never change the way I stride .

- Jagriti Tiwari

Acknowledgements

This collection of poems is not merely a gathering of words,

but a sacred offering of bonds, emotions, and memories
that kept the lamp of creation glowing within me.

*To my mother, **Mrs. Bharti Tiwari (1981),***
who wrapped me in the warmth of patience and strength
—
I remain forever indebted.

*To my father, **Mr. J.P. Tiwari (1973),***
whose shelter made every difficult path feel gentle,
it is his blessings that gave wings to my dreams.

*To my little blossom of a sister, **Omi Tiwari (2011),***
*and my radiant flame of a brother, **Rudra Tiwari (2015)**—*
your laughter and innocence are the sweetest melodies of my poems.

To my true friends,

M.V. Parul (2003) *and* ***Shweta Anand (2005)***,

whose trust and companionship urged me to keep writing—

you are the unspoken co-travelers of this journey.

It is their presence that breathes life into my words, and their love that forms the true foundation of this collection .

1. " The Actor ! "

Some say I'm a helping hand,
while others call me useless sand.

When I pour ink upon the page,
they say—"a poet, a man of stage."

If I speak of bonds, of trust, of cheer,
they sigh—what role is he playing here?

Yet time alone will one day decide,
what sort of actor in life I hide.

2. " The divine soul ! "

Be it called the day or night,
when you appear, the world feels right.

In every word, in every song,
your presence lingers all along.

Be I foolish, be I wise,
all my names in you arise.

If you say "yes," then yes I'll be,
if you say "no," then no for me.

Though fate may tear your hand from mine,
still I'll engrave your name divine.

If I should speak with all my heart,
I'd call you life, my sacred part.

My soul, my worship, all I own,
the truest light I've ever known.

And if one glance of you I gain,
the moon itself burns weak, in vain—
for even it would fade away,
a torch before your radiant sway.

3. " Moment ! "

A burning ache resides in me,
or I'm the last flame left to be.

The pain is more, the hope is slight,
from my own self I stand in flight.

A girl once dreamed with boundless skies ,
but now those dreams are shattered lies .

Perhaps some moments still remain,
or just one moment, lone, sustains.

4. " Chained Sky "

The walls are cracked, the chains are tight,
My sky lies captive, robbed of light.
Only a pen, a page remain,
To voice my sorrow, to bear my pain.

This touch alive, this wound unhealed,
A living ache I cannot shield.
Forget tomorrow—why pretend?
Even today feels too heavy to mend.

A window whispers from the side,
It calls each day, with hope inside.
Yet shadows blame the dark, not me,
That grips my soul relentlessly.

Whom do I tell? What can I say?
My age is half, my years still stray.
Rebellion burns within my core,
That's why my breaths still trickle more.

I never knew the stars above,
Upon my rug I spread my love.
Wrapped in white, that silent girl,
Why does the world reject her world?

A knock resounds upon the door,
It feels as if—someone once more?
She shrinks into a corner tight,
In nameless fear, or hidden spite.

A shadow looms of dread or blame,
She sighs relief when voices came.
A sound familiar, faint, yet near,
A breath of comfort through the fear.

She longs to reach, extend her hand,
But something stops her, makes her stand.
Her eyes lie dry, her chest confined,
A choking weight on heart and mind.

That girl who screams, who loudly cries,
Yet weeps unseen, with endless sighs.
It seems that fate has turned away,
Show mercy—she's too young today.

5. " I am only defeated by you ! "

You are my love, my endless fire,
Nothing is new, yet old desire.
Just one glance, one fleeting sight,
Say the word, I'll love with might.

How can I tell this storm inside?
One look from you, and worlds collide.
In my closed fist, the skies I'd keep,
For you, my love, my heart runs deep.

When you arrive, the springtime sings,
Your sorrow spreads a winter's wings.
I am the ocean, fierce and true,
You are the waterfall rushing through.

You're a qawwali, soulful, divine,
Or a thousand songs with your name entwined.
The world I conquered, yet you've won,
In your love, how many are undone?

You're verses written, sacred, bright,
A holy book I long to recite.
Pure is your soul, so vast, so true,
Before your grace, I turn to dew.

Temples and mosques the world may seek,
But I am defeated, humble, meek.
In you, my God, my faith I see,
My creed, my prayer begins with thee.

I write for you, for none but you,
You are my worship, my endless truth.
Lover, beggar, name me as you will,
I'm just your shadow, following still.

The world I've conquered, battles through,
Yet my heart surrenders... only to you .

6. " White ! "

Free from all deceit and lies,
In my own art, my beauty lies.
In every form, so pure, so real,
I am the color, complete, ideal.

I am the moon, I am the smile,
The proof of beauty all the while.
I blend within each shade, each hue,
Yet selfless in the love I strew.
A color of wonder, calm, divine,
In every heart, I choose to shine.

Beyond all colors, I stand apart,
With truth and purity in my heart.
The emblem of honesty, ever bright,
I am perfection, I am White.

From newborn's hands to final rest,
I cradle life, I calm the quest.
From shroud to grave, in love I stay,

A silent witness, pure as day.

I am the symbol of peace untold,
The finest color the world can hold.

7. " Life ! "

Restless, ruthless, aimless, wild,
Life is a storm, both fierce and mild.
No word can truly hold it tight,
Life owes no one, yet takes its right.

For something, it sings a fleeting song,
For something else, it sulks too long.
Silent in sorrow, loud in strife,
So strange, so stubborn, is this life.

How many colors has it drained,
How many hearts it has pained.
A rumor spreads through every street,
While rulers set their laws complete.

Yet in its tale, some truth is found,
A weight that makes the soul profound.
Perhaps this struggle, endlessly—
Is all that we call "Life" to be.

8. " Faith ! "

I've seen a thousand faces wear
Masks beyond compare.
I've watched integrity be sold,
For just a few coins of gold.

So young in age, yet wisdom deep,
I've seen glass fragments learn to keep
The weight of stone, the hardened face,
Fragile hearts turned into mace.

Desires, longings, fragile dreams,
Collided hard with truth's extremes.
I've seen the stars fall from the skies,
Shattered on earth before my eyes.

9. " Truth or lie ? "

What's the difference, tell me clear,
Between a face, and a soul sincere?

What line divides intent from sight,
The gaze that strays, the will that's right?

A petition's filed, the case is heard,
Against a leader, in court with words.

Now tell me, where does the difference lie,
Between the truth... and the perfect lie?

10. " Prayer ! "

I feel estranged from myself,
They say I have changed,
become someone unrecognizable.

My hands grow cold,
the body no longer obeys,
as if the darkness
has embraced me fully.

It seems I am but a guest of a few moments,
with nothing left to say,
destroyed by my own hands.

Friends, family—
why do they rush to save me now?
It feels like they hide
their own sins behind my fading breath.

Medicines have turned their face away,
perhaps I now hold

only the hands of prayers.

But even those raised hands
begin to tremble,
and the bowed head
grows weary too.

It feels as if my breath
is about to leave me.

The pen and ink—my oldest companions,
return to memory,
yet my story seems
too small to tell.

Dust has gathered thick,
and in this closed room,
light itself has grown dim.

11. " A Thread of Breath ! "

Life hangs on a fragile thread of breath—
twisting, turning, spinning, trembling,
endlessly swaying,
yet never breaking.

It feels as though someone cries inside—
an old house, heavy rains,
a vast suffocating darkness.
No one stands beside,
and man remains utterly alone.

I knocked on doors with all my strength,
yet was met with silence,
a sigh, and rejection.
It seemed someone had surrendered,
defeated by life itself.

Once, he too shared joy,
but now only darkness clings.
Is it a dying torch?

Or did he blow it out himself?

Who is this intruder
that lights the dark?
A stubborn spirit,
creeping through the broken window.

The floor beneath me is cold as stone,
a fan spins above,
its blades rattling from the ceiling.
I watch the shadows sway.

One could fall from the terrace,
or choose to die below.
Eyes flooding red with tears,
lips trembling with pain.

Still, fate's anger never ceases—
a punishment that grows,
a distance from death,
when death itself feels like a friend.

What more can I say?
This fragile thread of
breath
still rests
in the hands of destiny.

12. " Lady Love ! "

Is it some festival of delight,
That happiness walks with us tonight?

A sudden smile lit up your face,
Surely, a secret hides in its grace.

The steps once strayed to taverns afar,
Now turn back home, where heartbeats are.

This passion we nursed, this love we made,
Was costly enough, yet gladly paid.

It seems this time no parting stays,
The heart plays music, the soul obeys.

For lo—today, with radiant eyes,
The Lady Love herself arrives.

13. " Whispers in moonlight ! "

When I gaze a little closer, in the flowing breeze,
I see broken dreams, scattered with ease.

On faces, I notice silent complaints,
On faces, I notice hidden restraints.

Perhaps someone has lost their own,
Perhaps someone drifts far, alone.
Some search for someone they yearn,
Some are helpless at every turn.

Those veiled in secrecy's cover,
Also reveal truths they can't smother.

And I wonder—why do they only stare at the moon?
What grudge do they hold against the sun's boon?

Then I realize—the sorrow they keep,
They tie with the darkness, in silence so deep.

And the beloved they lost, so far,
They seek in moonlight's scattered star.

What wonder lies in the moon's embrace,
That every soul adores its face!

But truly, who would not be charmed?
Yes—within shattered lives, disarmed,
It grants a beautiful illusion still,
A fragile dream the heart can fill.

14. " The Dawn of Love ! "

One night,
that rainfall,
our very first meeting.

Just a few steps,
soft and slow...

She—drenched,
I—soaked,

She—shy,
I—trembling.

An odd silence lingered,
yet hearts drew closer.

Thus began—
the very first chapter of love.

15. " In your hands .... "

I am like an endless sea ,
You are my shore , my destiny .

Hold tight this fragile thread ,
in your hands my kite is led .

Buds may bloom in gardens wide,
Yet all my bending leans to your side.

If you choose me, blessed I'll be,
Think well, decide my fate with me.

For in your hands my life is tied,
Its reins, its course, its wings, its guide.

16. " The weight of Every Step ! "

On little things, so small, so slight,
I shed my tears in the quiet of night.

On baseless thoughts, I know not why,
I waste my moments as they pass me by.

In tangled webs of my own mind,
I lose long hours, no peace I find.

A hidden softness lives in me,
Perhaps it seeks its own calm sea.

I weave each tale with tender care,
And spend my time just lingering there.

Afraid someone may fool my trust,
This fear unsettles, shake me it must.

And so, at every step I stay,
Measuring, weighing—choosing the way.

17. " The Ocean's pearl...... "

Each time I dare to speak the truth,
The world will see it as uncouth.
But if I silence what burns inside,
A flame will smolder, never subside.

My soul is carved from self-respect,
Against each lie I shall object.
Their falsehoods rise, their tales ignite,
But my revolt will burn so bright.

And what of people, what they say?
Even when I am gone away,
Their murmurs linger, never cease,
Complaints will chase me past my peace.

Look closely, with a thoughtful eye—
No one is truly weak, or shy.
For loss and gain are passing streams,
No one is broken as it seems.

So better not to heed their cries,
For oceans hold the pearls they prize.
And still they say, with bitter art,
"How flawed it is, this ocean's heart."

18. " Ashes of love , Flames of words " !

Eyes run dry, the lips turn bare,
In ruins of life, no soul will care.
Until a kingdom of grief takes reign,
No poet is born from joy or gain.

What man is this, so strange, so still?
His eyes are dry, yet bleeds the will.
He hides his pain from every sight,
Collecting tears in the cloak of night.

Perhaps he dares not let it show,
The storm within, the silent woe.
So gathers sorrow, drop by drop,
A heart that breaks but will not stop.

Once every lover burned in flame,
Consumed by longing, without shame.
And when even modesty tore apart,
It carved deep wounds within the heart.

If not the moth, consumed at last,
Then what becomes of love so vast?

19. " Suicide note ! "

Today, dear Mother, I am yours,
Yet not the daughter I was before.

Clothed in silks, a radiant face,
A smile once bloomed–now lost its place.

I fear the world, its cruel disguise,
Its burning stares, its piercing whys–
Why were my garments torn apart?
Why crushed the flowers of my heart?
Why did my laughter fade to cries,
And drown in flames of silent skies?

Who will embrace you now, they say?
My kin, my blood, all turn away–
Mother, father, brother, kin,
Shamed, they hide the love within.

No matter how I try, O Ma,
The cries of pain still echo far.

Those screams, those wounds, they never cease,
My soul still pleads, it begs for peace.

Their shadows linger, touch remains,
Unwashed, unseen, eternal stains.
Where lay my fault? I cannot know,
Why did this fate betray me so?

Broken, I stand before your eyes,
I could not guard your sacred ties.
Now every breath feels hard to take,
My courage gone, my spirit breaks.

Forgive me, Mother—let me rest,
Your dearest child who failed the test.
For she, your daughter once so near,
Perhaps is gone, no longer here.

20. " Nameless - Melodies......."

I wrote myself into your name,
At dawn your breath, at dusk the same.
In secret streets where whispers fade,
I called you "nameless," yet love remained.

Not once, not twice—
But a hundred times,
I wrote myself into your name.

I know the weight of fleeting days,
How fate may bend, how hearts may change.
The wheel of time will pull apart,
What once was whole, it breaks the heart.

If you're the start, then I'm the end,
Your story lives where my verses blend.
In the diary of my songs and verses , line by line,
I penned every melody that calls you mine.

Again, again, in endless flame—
I wrote myself into your name.

21. " Longing in silence "

In the smallest words, the slightest things,
Lingered complaints, hidden stings.
While within, a storm was bound,
A silent tempest, without sound.

Someone yearned for a single bite,
Yet sold another's share outright.

So speak not of the path of love,
Where trials rise, the heavens above.

For there he stood, in patient wait,
Longing for a glimpse, at fate.

And in the shelter of those arms,
I found my friend, my heart's calm.

22. " Truth - death ! "

Yesterday, as I walked the lane,
a flying shroud crossed my domain.
It seemed a veil of sorrow's flight,
a soul departing into night.

I traced its path down to the shore,
where mourners gathered evermore.
Amidst the throng, a child I found,
his cries the only living sound.

And in those tears of tender years,
a sudden manhood first appears.
The rites were swift, the pyre was set,
a woman dressed in death I met.

The sight too heavy, grief too deep,
I placed the cloth her love to keep.
And turning home with burdened breath,
I'd seen the world, its truth, in death .

23. " The Silent Storm ! "

Why is this life a debt unpaid?
Is every account of fate truly made?

Why does fire burn within my chest?
Why hides a song in every rest?

Why does the sun still crown the sky?
And why must my own fall draw nigh?

What guard is placed upon the moon?
What secrets hide in night's cocoon?

Is something slipping out of me?
Why do my breaths grow faint, unfree?

Is what I see the final shore?
Or lies my fate in stars elsewhere, in more?

Whom am I fighting, what unseen root?
Where lies the origin of this dispute?

They ask me, Who are you, say?
How can I answer—when I am silence, clay?

The roads are haunted with straying turns,
My chest weighed down with silent burns.

Do pains too have their strings and lyres?
If so, why mute are the cries it inspires?

When I question myself alone,
How can I speak what I've never known?

For there is a storm within my quiet,
And deep unrest within my riot.

Each step I take, I drift apart—
Yet inside, I'm breaking, heart by heart.

24. " Broken Wings ! "

With half-torn wings, confused, afraid,
The dove sits helpless, dismayed.
Shattered and broken, steeped in despair,
A hopeless silence lingers there.

Feather by feather, he tries to mend,
To dress his wings, to hope again.
Is he mending wounds, or weaving dreams?
Building his sky from broken seams?

Pearls of tears fall from his eyes,
His beak still struggles, never denies.
In restless haste he moves about,
Or hides from truth, so harsh, so loud.

What vision struck, what scene so grim?
That even the heart grew weak within.

But a bird without wings cannot survive,
As man without breath is not alive.

And though he tried with all his might,
The dove could not reclaim his flight.
This tale of loss is not just his—

It speaks of every life like this.

www.ingramcontent.com/pod-product-compliance
Lightning Source LLC
LaVergne TN
LVHW022030200926
848481LV00007B/2629
9798900810652